The Gypsy Moth And How To Control It

Leland Ossian Howard

In the interest of creating a more extensive selection of rare historical book reprints, we have chosen to reproduce this title even though it may possibly have occasional imperfections such as missing and blurred pages, missing text, poor pictures, markings, dark backgrounds and other reproduction issues beyond our control. Because this work is culturally important, we have made it available as a part of our commitment to protecting, preserving and promoting the world's literature. Thank you for your understanding.

28,636

Issued January 18, 1907.

U. S. DEPARTMENT OF AGRICULTURE.

FARMERS' BULLETIN 275.

THE GIPSY MOTH AND HOW TO CONTROL IT

BY

L. O. HOWARD,
ENTOMOLOGIST.

WASHINGTON:
GOVERNMENT PRINTING OFFICE.
1907.

LETTER OF TRANSMITTAL.

UNITED STATES DEPARTMENT OF AGRICULTURE,
BUREAU OF ENTOMOLOGY,
Washington, D. C., December 14, 1906.

SIR: I have the honor to transmit a brief account of the gipsy moth (*Porthetria dispar*), with some consideration of methods of control, which I believe is suited for publication as a Farmers' Bulletin.

Respectfully,
L. O. HOWARD,
Entomologist and Chief of Bureau.

Hon. JAMES WILSON,
Secretary of Agriculture.

CONTENTS.

	Page.
Introduction	7
The gipsy moth in Europe	7
Introduction into America and subsequent spread	8
The territory now infested in the United States	10
Massachusetts	10
New Hampshire	11
Maine	11
Rhode Island	11
Connecticut	11
Description of the insect	12
The eggs	12
The larva or caterpillar	12
The pupa	13
The adult or moth	13
Seasonal history	13
How the insect spreads	14
Damage to plants	15
Natural enemies and parasites	15
Remedies	16
What the State of Massachusetts is doing for the control of the insect	19
Features of the Massachusetts law	19
The moths are public nuisances	19
The superintendent of suppression	19
Duties of cities, towns, and individuals	19
Notice to private owners	19
Failure of private owners to destroy moths	20
Redress by abatement and appeal	20
Appropriation by the Commonwealth	20
Reimbursements to cities and towns	20
Limits to required expenditure by cities and towns	20
Valuations of 1904 taken as basis	21
Willful resistance or obstruction	21
What other States hope to do	21
What the National Government is doing	21

ILLUSTRATIONS.

	Page
FIG. 1. Districts in Massachusetts infested by the gipsy moth in 1900 and 1905..	9
2. Egg mass of the gipsy moth (*Porthetria dispar*)	12
3. Full-grown caterpillar of the gipsy moth	12
4. Pupa of the gipsy moth	12
5. Male gipsy moth	13
6. Female gipsy moth	13
7. Manner of applying burlap bands	17

THE GIPSY MOTH AND HOW TO CONTROL IT.

INTRODUCTION.

The gipsy moth (*Porthetria dispar* L.) is an European insect which was accidentally introduced into Massachusetts nearly forty years ago and has since spread rather slowly, being still confined to the eastern part of Massachusetts, to Rhode Island, to the southern part of New Hampshire, and to more or less isolated localities in eastern Connecticut and southwestern Maine.

After the discovery of its presence, in 1889, the State of Massachusetts for a number of years kept up a vigorous effort to exterminate the insect, and this effort was supported by large appropriations, but was abandoned in 1900. In 1905 appropriations were again made for the purpose of attempting to suppress this insect and the brown-tail moth,[a] and these appropriations are still in operation.

Although appealed to on several occasions, the National Government took no steps to assist the State of Massachusetts in its fight against this destructive species—with the exception of a small appropriation made in 1905 for the purpose of introducing its natural enemies—until the present year. At the first session of the Fifty-ninth Congress, however, the sum of $82,500 was appropriated, to be expended by the Secretary of Agriculture, through the Bureau of Entomology, in an effort to prevent the further spread of the gipsy moth and the brown-tail moth. Under this appropriation active work is now going on in parts of New England, and the character of this work is explained in a later section of this bulletin. A popular consideration of the brown-tail moth has been published in Farmers' Bulletin No. 264, and the present bulletin is planned for the purpose of presenting in concise form what is known at the present time about the gipsy moth.

THE GIPSY MOTH IN EUROPE.

The gipsy moth has a wide distribution throughout middle and southern Europe, western Asia, and northern Africa, reaching from Stockholm on the north to Algiers on the south, and to England on the west. It extends across to eastern Asia, including Japan, and

---

[a] See Farmers' Bulletin No. 264, U. S. Dept. Agric., 1906.

has been found in Ceylon. In a large portion of its European range the gipsy moth is occasionally abundant and injurious; but these injurious outbreaks occur only at intervals, and in many portions of its range it becomes noticeable only very rarely. For the most part, it is satisfactorily held in check by its natural enemies.

INTRODUCTION INTO AMERICA AND SUBSEQUENT SPREAD.

Unlike the brown-tail moth, the precise time and method of introduction of the gipsy moth is well known. Prof. Leopold Trouvelot, in 1869, was connected with the astronomical observatory at Harvard University, and, for his pleasure and interest, was engaged at odd times in the study of wild silkworms, with the idea that species of commercial value might be found, and that perhaps something might be done in the way of cross breeding to produce a hardier insect than the silkworm of commerce, and one which, perhaps, might prove to be resistant to the pebrine disease which at that time was playing havoc in the silkworm establishments of Europe. He imported different silk-spinning caterpillars in different stages of existence, and among others egg clusters of the gipsy moth. He lived at 27 Myrtle street, Medford, and raised caterpillars on a shrub in his dooryard, inclosing them with a net. During a gale the net was torn and the insects scattered. He searched for them, and destroyed those found; he also gave notice of the probable escape of the species, but the affair was soon forgotten. For many years the insect was not noticed by the people of Medford, and it probably increased very slowly. It is supposed that it was gradually accommodating itself to the climate, and it is known that the neighborhood abounded with insectivorous birds and that adjoining wood lots were frequently burned over. Eventually the insect became noticeable, and by the summer of 1889 had multiplied to such an extent as to become a notorious pest; then for the first time specimens were sent to the State agricultural experiment station at Amherst and determined by Dr. H. T. Fernald as the well-known gipsy moth of Europe.

The town of Medford raised a sum of money to fight the insect, and in the spring of 1890 the State appropriated $25,000, an additional $25,000 being appropriated early in June. Other appropriations followed from year to year with gradually increasing amounts, and admirable work was done under the Massachusetts State board of agriculture by Mr. E. H. Forbush in charge of the field operations, and Prof. C. H. Fernald in charge of the scientific and technical work. The last appropriation was expended in 1899, and the legislature refused to vote further sums for 1900 and the following years. In 1905 the appropriations were renewed, and the work has since been carried on under a well-founded State law, the provisions of which are summarized in the concluding section of this bulletin.

The accompanying map (fig. 1) indicates accurately the infested district of Massachusetts at the time of the interruption of the State work in 1900. It also shows the district found infested in 1906, when the work of suppression was recommenced by the State. The interruption of the work is thus seen to have been almost disastrous. In

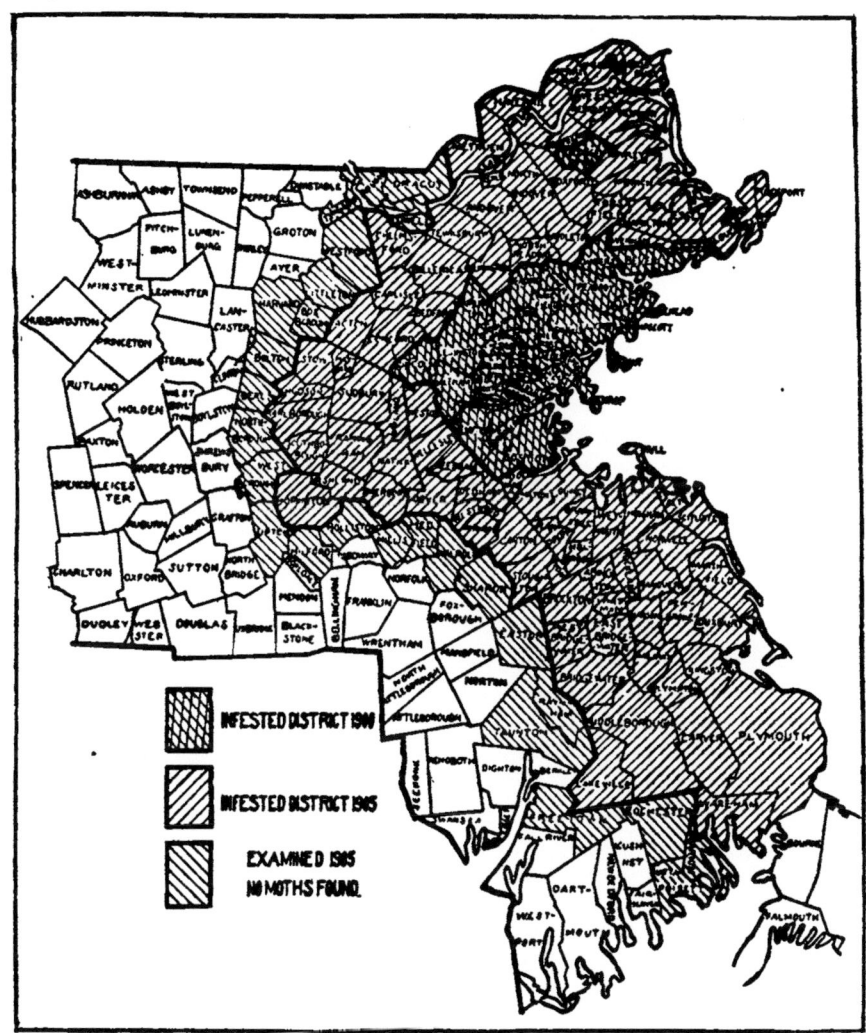

FIG. 1.—Districts in Massachusetts infested by the gipsy moth in 1900 and 1905. Infested area in 1900, 359 square miles; in 1905, 2,224 square miles. (From Kirkland.)

1899 the State board of agriculture had the problem well in hand, and at that time it seemed very probable to skilled practical entomologists who looked into the matter that even extermination was possible in the course of a comparatively short time. But the five years' interruption of the work caused the spread of the insect from a restricted territory of 359 square miles throughout an extended range of 2,224 square miles. Beyond the limit indicated as that of 1905 the moth has probably not spread to any very great extent within the limits of the State of Massachusetts. Scouting work, however, during the early spring of 1906 and the autumn of the same year has indicated a general spread over the New Hampshire border into the southern tier of counties of that State, and recent scouting in Maine has shown the establishment of the gipsy moth at several points in the southwestern portion of that State. Moreover, it has been found near Stonington, Conn., and over a considerable space within and about the city of Providence, R. I.

THE TERRITORY NOW INFESTED IN THE UNITED STATES.

The territory at present infested may be briefly considered by States as follows:

Massachusetts.—The gipsy moth has been found in Massachusetts by the local State force in 138 cities and towns, which represent an area of about 2,480 square miles. The most seriously infested section is a group of about twenty towns just north of Boston, including a territory surrounded by Salem, Peabody, Lynnfield, Wakefield, Stoneham, Woburn, Lexington, Waltham, Watertown, and Cambridge. Within this territory almost every tree is more or less infested. Thousands of fruit trees and shade trees have been killed by this pest; in the woodlands one can easily find blocks of from 1 to 50 acres in which almost every tree is dead. During the past summer several thousand acres of these woodlands were entirely denuded of foliage. The voracious feeding of the gipsy-moth caterpillars year after year must soon cause the loss of other large areas of woodland.

Outside the badly infested area mentioned above the gipsy moth occurs in less alarming numbers, until in some of the outside towns it is only discovered after a most careful search.

The territory to the south of Boston, except the city of Quincy, is not known to be infested to a serious extent, although the moth has been discovered south to Buzzards Bay and east to Orleans. In most of the towns in this southern district there are from three or four to one hundred or more colonies. While no serious damage has yet resulted from the presence of the moth in this section of the State, the infestations are there, and unless strenuous measures are resorted to this territory will in a few years be devastated as severely as has been the country to the north of Boston.

The country to the west and north of the badly infested central region, while quite seriously infested in spots, shows the moth in decreasing numbers as we diverge from this center. The infestation extends as far west as Westboro and Ayer and north all along the New Hampshire border.

Under the State laws of Massachusetts and through its liberal appropriations, the trees on the streets and in the residential sections of the cities and towns have received sufficient attention to prevent any serious damage this year.

New Hampshire.—In New Hampshire the presence of the gipsy moth in small numbers was known in the autumn of 1905 in all of the seacoast towns and in the city of Portsmouth, but little systematic work was done until August of this year, since which time employees of the Bureau of Entomology have discovered the moth widely scattered in eight towns, which are all that have been thoroughly scouted. This territory includes Greenland, Portsmouth, Seabrook, Hampton Falls, North Hampton, and Rye. Effective scouting, however, can be done only after the leaves fall, and that now going on will probably reveal the presence of the insect over a much larger area.

Maine.—During the early autumn the gipsy moth was reported in Kittery, Me., since which time a careful scout has been made of Kittery, Eliot, and York, in all of which towns the insect has been discovered, with the probability that it will be found in other towns. Systematic scouting work is being continued in this State.

Rhode Island.—The gipsy moth was discovered in Providence, R. I., in 1901, and during that summer the city made some effort toward its eradication. From 1901 to 1906 very little work was done, and during that period the moth has spread until it now abounds in nearly every portion of the city, occurring in the largest numbers in the northeastern and southwestern sections. It has spread also into the adjoining towns of Cranston and Johnston.

There are several small but very bad colonies in Providence, some of which show infestation almost equal to the badly infested places in Massachusetts. Most of the known infestation is confined to city property, and, unless large colonies of the moth are discovered in the woodlands, a continued, aggressive campaign should result in the extermination of the pest in this territory.

Connecticut.—In the summer of 1905 the gipsy moth was discovered in Stonington, Conn., and, so far as known, it is confined to an area of about 1 square mile to the north and east of Stonington Village. During the winter of 1905 and 1906 some 60 or 70 egg clusters were destroyed; during the past summer trees were burlaped, several acres of brush land cut over, some of the stone walls burned out, and the moth vigorously hunted by the State authorities under direction of Doctor Britton. Since the egg-laying season of the past summer about 40 more egg clusters were destroyed. Unless an examination of the surrounding territory should reveal the moth over a much larger area, this colony should be entirely stamped out within a year or two, although it will require careful watching for several seasons to be sure that it does not reestablish itself.

DESCRIPTION OF THE INSECT.

The eggs.—The eggs of the gipsy moth are laid in masses (fig. 2) of about five hundred. The individual egg is minute, about the size of a pinhead, and is salmon-colored when first laid, but turns dark in the

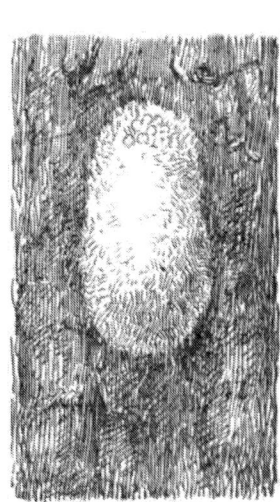

Fig. 2.—Egg mass of the gipsy moth (*Porthetria dispar*). (From Kirkland.)

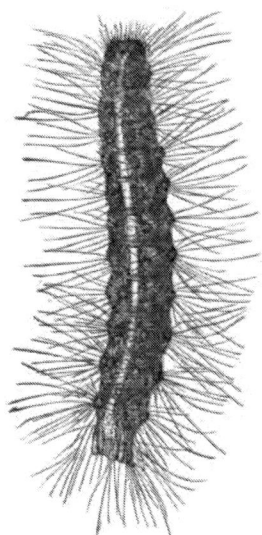

Fig. 3.—Full-grown caterpillar of the gipsy moth. Natural size (from Insect Life).

course of a few weeks. Each egg mass is yellowish in appearance and seems covered with hair. It is somewhat oval, being one-half of an inch long and about three-fourths of an inch wide. During winter,

Fig. 4.—Pupa of gipsy moth. Natural size (from Insect Life).

from exposure to moisture in the atmosphere, it becomes dingy white in color.

The larva or caterpillar.—The young larvæ or young caterpillars are dark in color and well furnished with dark hairs. The full-grown larva (fig. 3) is between 2 and 3 inches long, dark brown or sooty in color, with two rows of red spots and two rows of blue spots along the back, and with a yellowish but rather dim stripe between them. The body generally is clothed with long hairs, and sometimes reaches the length of 3 inches.

The pupa.—The pupa (fig. 4) is not inclosed within a perfect cocoon, but the full-grown larva spins a few threads of silk as a sort of support and changes to the pupa, which is dark reddish or chocolate in color and very thinly sprinkled with light reddish hairs.

The adult or moth.—The male moth (fig. 5) is brownish yellow in color, sometimes having a greenish-brown tinge; it has a slender body, well-feathered antennæ, and a wing expanse of about an inch and a half. The forewings are marked with wavy zigzag darker lines. It flies actively all day as well as by night.

FIG. 5.—Male gipsy moth. Slightly enlarged (from Insect Life).

FIG. 6.—Female gipsy moth. Slightly enlarged (from Insect Life).

The female moth (fig. 6) is nearly white, with slender black antennæ, each of the forewings marked with three or four zigzag, transverse, dark lines, and the outer border of both pairs of wings with a series of black dots. The body of the female is so heavy as to prevent flight.

SEASONAL HISTORY.

The moths emerge from the pupæ from the middle of July to the middle of August, the date varying considerably according to the season. After mating they live but a short time, and the female dies after depositing her eggs.

The eggs are laid therefore in July and August. They are deposited by the moths on the trunks of the trees upon which the caterpillars have lived, and in fact usually in the vicinity of the place where the female has transformed. The caterpillars before transforming frequently crawl for some distance from the trees upon which they have been feeding, and it therefore happens that the egg masses will be found on fences and in all sorts of protected situations in which the caterpillars hide during the day. The crevices in stone fences often contain very many of these egg masses, and knot holes in old trees will also contain many which would not at first be discovered. The egg masses are found also in hollow trees, in crevices under rough bark, on shrubbery, on buildings, in wood piles, in barrels, in boxes, and among rubbish in dooryards. The moths seem to choose the inner or lower surface of an object upon which to lay their eggs, and therefore egg masses are placed out of sight perhaps as often as in sight.

The eggs hatch about May 1, and the young caterpillars begin immediately to feed, usually upon the lower surfaces of the leaves. As they grow they cast their skins several times, and as they become larger they feed only at night, hiding during the daytime, usually in clusters on the shady side of tree trunks, beneath large limbs, in holes in trees, under loose bark, and in fact under any nearby shelter. It is the habit of most of them to descend before daybreak upon the trunks of the trees and to seek for such shelters as those just indicated, returning after nightfall to resume their nocturnal feeding.

The larvæ usually become full grown about the 1st of July, and then transform to pupæ. The pupæ are found in the same situations as those we described for the egg clusters, but are found also in the foliage of trees and shrubs.

HOW THE INSECT SPREADS.

As indicated above, the bodies of the females are so heavy as to prevent flight. Therefore the insect must be principally distributed while in the caterpillar or larval condition. The caterpillars are active crawlers, but as a rule do not migrate from the localities where they were born except when food is scarce. When young, and when there is hardly enough food, the larvæ spin down from trees by means of silken threads and often alight upon vehicles of one kind or another, and are thus carried often for great distances from the place of birth. Trolley cars, carriages, automobiles, and bicycles are thus means of transportation almost unlimited in their possibilities. The caterpillars often crawl upon vehicles which happen to stand for any length of time in an infested locality, and thus may be carried great distances. Sometimes even pedestrians aid unwittingly in this distribution, since the caterpillars may drop by their threads upon the garments of a person passing under an infested tree.

The species may be transported, too, in the egg stage. It has been shown that the egg clusters are laid upon many different kinds of objects. Cord wood stacked and piled may be carried away in the autumn bearing many egg masses, and, if not burned before summer, larvæ may issue in a new locality. The same may be said for lumber piles near infested trees. Freight cars may have been sidetracked near an infested place long enough to permit laying of the eggs upon them.

It is by these methods that the comparatively rapid spread of the insect previously noticed, during the years 1900–1905, is to be explained.

DAMAGE TO PLANTS.

The larva of the gipsy moth feeds upon the foliage of practically all orchard trees, all shade and ornamental trees, all out-of-door shrubs, and all forest trees. Not only are the deciduous forest trees stripped, but the coniferous trees as well. In June and July patches of forests in the infested territory are stripped of every green leaf and the trees appear as bare as in winter. After several such consecutive strippings, deciduous forest and shade trees are killed, but with a coniferous tree, such as a pine, hemlock, or spruce, one complete stripping will cause death. It is this fact which makes the gipsy moth so much more serious a pest than the brown-tail moth, and the loss which will result from its spread into northern New England will be very great, owing to the enormous coniferous forest interests in that part of the country.

In cities and towns the insect does damage not only by destroying all vegetation, but by swarming in numbers upon and about houses, frequently entering them. It has been the experience in eastern Massachusetts that where a locality becomes thoroughly infested the value of real estate rapidly depreciates, and it becomes a matter of difficulty to rent or sell property.

Among its food plants the gipsy moth caterpillar seems to prefer apple, white oak, red oak, willow, and elm, but those who have studied it most carefully in Massachusetts say that it will on occasion devour almost every useful grass, plant, flower, shrub, vine, bush, garden, or field crop that grows in the State.

NATURAL ENEMIES AND PARASITES.

Observations extending over a number of years show that birds have some importance as enemies of the gipsy moth. As already suggested, the fact that the insects spread comparatively slowly in the vicinity of Medford between the years 1869 and 1889 is probably to be accounted for in part by the fact that insectivorous birds were much more numerous in that part of Massachusetts during that period than they have been since. Not only have the English sparrows (which, by the way, feed but rarely upon the gipsy moth) driven away many of the other birds, but pot-hunters from Boston and from the manufacturing towns about Boston, especially persons of foreign birth, have destroyed great numbers of insectivorous birds. The caterpillars are preyed upon by the cuckoos, the Baltimore oriole, the yellow-throated vireo, and the blue jay. The moths, when they emerge, are eaten by many birds, and the eggs are eaten by several species.

Certain of our native parasites which destroy allied insects like the fall webworm and the tussock moth also breed in the gipsy moth caterpillar and chrysalis. A number of species were bred during the early Massachusetts State work, but the percentage of parasitism was very small.

An effort is being made by the Bureau of Entomology, in cooperation with the Massachusetts State authorities, to introduce the European parasites of the gipsy moth, and of the brown-tail moth as well, and during the past year many thousands of such parasites have been introduced and liberated in the vicinity of Boston. They are first cared for in a laboratory at North Saugus; many of them are afterwards studied under out-of-door tents, while still others have been liberated in the open and badly infested woodlands, such locations for liberation having been chosen as are likely to remain undisturbed either by insecticidal operations or by forest fires. The results so far are encouraging, but it may be, and probably will be, several years before appreciable results will be obtained, and it may be that these European parasites will not increase as rapidly or do as good work as they are known to do in Europe. In the Old World, as has been previously indicated, the gipsy moth is only occasionally present in sufficient numbers to do noteworthy damage, and it is ordinarily kept in check by its parasites and other natural enemies. In this country, therefore, active mechanical measures must still be continued, and perhaps for years to come, in the actual destruction of the injurious insect before relief from parasites is gained.

REMEDIES.

The gipsy moth, when occurring in moderate numbers, is not at all a difficult insect to fight. When young the caterpillars are readily killed by spraying the trees with the ordinary arsenical poisons. As they grow older they develop a remarkable resistance to the action of arsenic, so that stronger and stronger proportions must be used. It was early found that Paris green and London purple can not be used effectively against well-grown larvæ unless the proportion of the arsenical to the amount of water is so great as to burn the foliage of the trees or plants. Therefore the substance known as arsenate of lead, which admits of much stronger proportions without damage to foliage, was introduced and has since been extensively used, not only against the well-grown gipsy moth larvæ, but against other leaf-eating insects.

But against the larger larvæ other measures may be used to advantage. It has been pointed out that it is the habit of the larvæ to descend upon the trunk of the tree in the early morning and to hide under any protection until nightfall. Therefore, if a strip of burlap or other coarse, cheap cloth is tied about an infested tree trunk by the middle, in such a manner that the flaps hang down (see fig. 7), the caterpillars, as soon as they have reached this stage, will gather for the day under the cloth and can be destroyed by crushing or cutting. The burlap should be examined daily, and may be employed from the latter half of May to the first or middle of August—as late as the latter date, for the reason that many caterpillars transform to pupæ under the burlap and many egg masses are also laid under it. As Kirkland has well expressed it, "It should be borne in mind that the cloth band is in no sense a tree protector; nor is it a trap. Its function is simply to give the shelter which the caterpillars seek by day. Serving as it does as a hiding place for various insects, it is better off the tree than on unless it can be attended to and kept clean. At the end of the caterpillar season all burlaps should be removed and burned. To insure best results on high trees, such as street elms, burlaps should be placed around some of the larger limbs, as well as around the trunk, as many caterpillars will seek shelter up in the tree rather than descend to the ground. The most effective results in using the burlap are obtained where cavities, crevices, etc., in the trees have been first filled with cement or covered with zinc and all loose bark removed. If these hiding places are destroyed nearly all the caterpillars will seek the burlap at some time during the season."

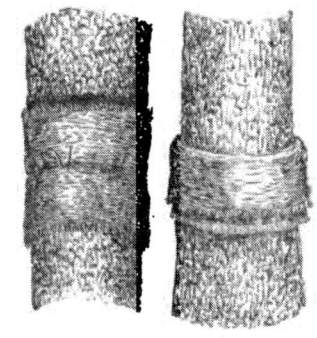

FIG. 7.—Manner of applying burlap bands: a, band as originally tied; b, band with upper half turned down. Greatly reduced (after Forbush).

One of the most effective methods of destruction consists in killing the eggs. The egg masses are often conspicuous and accessible and may be destroyed by applying creosote mixtures by a small swab or paint brush. This mixture may be bought at agricultural warehouses and seed stores at from 50 cents to $1 a gallon. Every egg mass thus treated means the destruction of 500 potential caterpillars. The egg clusters should be creosoted early in the autumn if possible, since they are likely to be broken and the eggs scattered on the ground by the rubbing of animals against the trees, or by the breaking open of the clusters by cats and squirrels, or by the picking of birds, thus also scattering the eggs. Much good can also be accomplished by burning over unimproved tracts of brush land and burning out the undergrowth in sparse woodlands. Where the clusters are very plentiful, burning the ground over with oil to destroy eggs scattered as the result of the cutting of trees and bushes will, according to Kirkland, be required to insure thorough work. The burning method is also effective in May or June, after the young larvæ have hatched.

With the creosoting of the eggs, the spraying against the young larvæ, the burlaping against the old larvæ, and with burning in places indicated, the insect may be kept in check. So great, however, is the prolificacy of the species, and in such enormous numbers does it occur in eastern Massachusetts, that the thorough use of these and other methods of destruction upon a large estate involves a great expenditure of money. For example, Gen. S. C. Lawrence for a number of years kept a large force of men working upon certain gipsy moth colonies in his own and adjoining forest lands, and expended each year more than the actual value of the lands. This experience, however, need not and should not discourage small property holders from vigorous efforts to destroy the insects upon their own holdings. Unless extraordinarily abundant, it is perfectly feasible to hold them in check.

One of the most serious features of the damage is the injury in park lands in eastern Massachusetts, where thousands of acres are infested and where important problems exist. From long experience the best methods for treating these wooded sections have been proven to be the cutting out and burning of all underbrush, the removal of trees which have died or have inaccessible cavities in them, and the burning of all refuse on the ground. It is almost impossible to inspect the thick growths of underbrush for the various stages of the moth, and there is no method for their treatment at a reasonable cost. Trees which have been scarred by forest fires, or from other causes, often have cavities in them which provide admirable hiding places for these insects, and should be removed to prevent the constant expense of inspection.

Apple orchards, also, aside from those receiving the most careful attention, offer favorable breeding places for the moth. There are in New England thousands of old, badly infested apple trees which have passed their usefulness for producing good fruit, and the ground which they occupy might better be devoted to other crops or to newly set orchards. The field force rarely goes into an orchard that has not several trees with holes in them which might harbor the gipsy moth so safely that its presence could not be detected unless the tree were cut open. Such trees, if not worth being cared for by cementing or tinning the holes to prevent the entrance and exit of the gipsy moth, should be cut and burned.

Hedges of brush along roadsides and stone walls also offer favorable breeding and hiding places for the pest. In such places the presence of the moth may not be discovered for several years, the caterpillars feeding upon the brush and nesting in stone walls until the colony has developed to sufficient size to attract attention by its depredations on neighboring trees, upon which its presence is easily discovered. The cutting and burning of these rows of worthless shrubbery each year until killed not only removes a favorite hiding place for various insect pests, but also gives the roadside and farm a much more trim appearance.

WHAT THE STATE OF MASSACHUSETTS IS DOING FOR THE CONTROL OF THE INSECT.

In the session of the Massachusetts legislature in the spring of 1905 a law was passed which had for its object the suppression of the gipsy and brown tail moths. The essential features of this law are as follows:

FEATURES OF THE MASSACHUSETTS LAW.

The moths are public nuisances.—The gipsy and brown tail moths are declared public nuisances and their suppression is required.

The superintendent of suppression.—A superintendent appointed by the governor with power, subject to the governor's approval, of appointing agents and assistants has entire general charge of the work of suppressing the moths.

Duties of cities, towns, and individuals.—Cities and towns (under the advice and general direction of the superintendent, and by such agent as they may designate or appoint) are required, under penalty for neglect, to destroy the eggs, pupæ, and nests of the gipsy and the brown-tail moths within their limits, *excepting* that such work is not to be done by cities and towns on property controlled by the Commonwealth, nor is it to be done upon private property, excepting where the owners of the same fail to destroy the eggs, pupæ, and nests of the moths, in accordance with the terms of the official notice to private owners noted in the section here following:

Notice to private owners.—The mayor of every city and the selectmen of every town shall, at suitable times, notify every owner of land located therein which is infested with the moths, requiring him to destroy the eggs, pupæ, and nests of the moths within a specified time.

When the mayor or selectmen decide that the cost of such destruction (on lands contiguous and under one ownership) will exceed one-half of 1 per cent of the assessed valuation of the lands, then they may designate in the notice a part only of such lands on which the destruction shall take place.

Failure of private owners to destroy moths.—If the owner does not, as required by the terms of the aforesaid notice, destroy the eggs, pupæ, and nests of the moths, then the city or town, subject to the approval of the State superintendent, shall destroy them, and shall assess upon such aforesaid lands the actual cost of so doing, to an amount, however, not exceeding one-half of 1 per cent of the assessed valuation of the land.

This amount, so assessed, shall be collected in the form of taxes, and constitutes a lien upon such lands.

Redress by abatement and appeal.—The assessors may abate the moth assessment in the case of any private landowner decided by them to be unable to pay it because of age, infirmity, or poverty.

Appeal to the county superior court, with special provision for prompt hearing, is provided by the statute for any person aggrieved by assessment on account of this work; provided a complaint is entered within 30 days of notice of such assessment.

Appropriation by the Commonwealth.—To meet the expenses incurred under its moth-suppression law the Commonwealth has appropriated $300,000. Of this sum $75,000 may be expended during 1905, $150,000 (and any unexpended balance) during 1906, and $75,000 (and any unexpended balance) during 1907, up to May 1, 1907, inclusive.

For the purpose of experimenting with natural enemies for destroying the moths, $10,000 is additionally appropriated for each of the years 1905, 1906, and 1907.

Reimbursements to cities and towns.—(1) Cities and towns with valuation of real and personal estate of $12,500,000 or more, having spent $5,000 in any one calendar year, shall be reimbursed annually 50 per cent (one-half) of all further expenditure in combating this pest.

(2) Cities and towns with valuation less than $12,500,000 and more than $6,000,000, having spent an amount equal to one twenty-fifth of 1 per cent of such valuation in one year, shall be reimbursed annually 80 per cent (four-fifths) of all further expenditure.

(3) Towns with valuation less than $6,000,000, having spent an amount equal to one twenty-fifth of 1 per cent of such valuation in one year, shall be reimbursed once in 60 days for all further expenditure.

Limits to required expenditure by cities and towns.—No city or town with an assessed real and personal valuation of more than $6,000,000 shall be required to expend in the suppression of the moths during any one full year more than one-fifteenth of 1 per cent of such valuation. No town with an assessed real and personal valuation of less than $6,000,000 shall be required to thus expend during any one full year more than one twenty-fifth of 1 per cent of such valuation.

Valuations of 1904 taken as basis.—Wherever valuations of real and personal property are referred to in the law for the suppression of the gipsy and brown-tail moth the valuations of 1904 are meant.

Willful resistance or obstruction.—Willful resistance to or obstruction of any agent of the Commonwealth or of any city or town, while lawfully engaged in the execution of the purposes of the moth-suppression law, is forbidden under penalty.

Under this law, Mr. A. H. Kirkland, a very well equipped man, was appointed superintendent, organized an effective force, and during the seasons of 1905 and 1906 has done excellent work. The experiences of these two years have shown certain defects in the law, which it is hoped will be remedied at the coming session of the State legislature.

WHAT OTHER STATES HOPE TO DO.

The comparatively recent spread of the gipsy moth into the States of New Hampshire, Connecticut, Rhode Island, and Maine, as indicated in an earlier paragraph of this bulletin, has created great public interest in these States, and at the coming sessions of the legislatures efforts will be made in each State to secure the passage of a law based upon the Massachusetts State law summarized above. In the meantime the State of Rhode Island has expended a certain amount of money appropriated by the legislature last winter, and the State of Connecticut has used certain funds at the disposal of the Director of the State agricultural experiment station. In New Hampshire and Maine no State work has yet been done.

WHAT THE NATIONAL GOVERNMENT IS DOING.

Congress at its last session appropriated, as elsewhere stated, the sum of $82,500 to be expended in an effort to prevent the further spread of the gipsy moth and the brown-tail moth. This money became available July 1, 1906, so that it was impossible to perfect the organization of the work in time to attempt any extended measures against the caterpillars this season. Mr. D. M. Rogers, formerly Mr. Kirkland's first assistant, was appointed special agent of the Bureau of Entomology in charge of the field work, a force of inspectors and laborers was organized, and work was begun about the middle of July.

After looking over the whole field and discussing the question at length with Messrs. Kirkland and Rogers, the writer concluded that since it seems obvious that nearly all of the recent spread of the gipsy moth has taken place by means of vehicles coming from the interior of the most thickly infested regions, the most effective manner of preventing further extensive spread would be to clean up the main traveled roads in the most thickly infested portions of the old gipsy-moth territory. The main work, therefore, was begun in the State of Massachusetts, and forces of men were placed on the principal infested roads to clean the shade trees and the underbrush for some distance back from the roads, in order that there may be no opportunity the coming season for caterpillars to spin down upon vehicles or passers-by, and thus to be carried to distances.

By cooperation with the State authorities in Rhode Island and Connecticut an effort has been made to stamp out the isolated colonies in these two States. This work has been actively carried on throughout the year, the Bureau paying for the services of the laborers and controlling their work in Rhode Island, but in the Connecticut case leaving affairs in charge of the State authorities.

Scouting parties have been and are working in New Hampshire and Maine in the effort accurately to map every infested point in order that all isolated colonies may be destroyed.

All of this work will be continued until the close of the fiscal year, and afterward provided Congress shall renew the appropriation.

The Government field office for gipsy-moth work is at No. 6 Beacon street, Boston, Mass., and the special field agent in charge is Mr. D. M. Rogers.

FARMERS' BULLETINS.

The following is a list of the Farmers' Bulletins available for distribution, showing the number, title, and size in pages of each. Copies will be sent free to any address in the United States on application to a Senator, Representative, or Delegate in Congress, or to the Secretary of Agriculture, Washington, D. C. Numbers omitted have been discontinued, being superseded by later bulletins.

22. The Feeding of Farm Animals. Pp. 40.
24. Hog Cholera and Swine Plague. Pp. 16.
25. Peanuts: Culture and Uses. Pp. 24.
27. Flax for Seed and Fiber. Pp. 16.
28. Weeds; and How to Kill Them. Pp. 32.
29. Souring and Other Changes in Milk. Pp. 22.
30. Grape Diseases on the Pacific Coast. Pp. 15.
32. Silos and Silage. Pp. 32.
33. Peach Growing for Market. Pp. 24.
34. Meats: Composition and Cooking. Pp. 29.
35. Potato Culture. Pp. 24.
36. Cotton Seed and Its Products. Pp. 16.
37. Kafir Corn: Culture and Uses. Pp. 12.
39. Onion Culture. Pp. 31.
41. Fowls: Care and Feeding. Pp. 24.
42. Facts About Milk. Pp. 32.
44. Commercial Fertilizers. Pp. 38.
46. Irrigation in Humid Climates. Pp. 27.
47. Insects Affecting the Cotton Plant. Pp. 32.
48. The Manuring of Cotton. Pp. 16.
49. Sheep Feeding. Pp. 24.
51. Standard Varieties of Chickens. Pp. 48.
52. The Sugar Beet. Pp. 48.
54. Some Common Birds. Pp. 48.
55. The Dairy Herd. Pp. 30.
56. Experiment Station Work—I. Pp. 31.
58. The Soy Bean as a Forage Crop. Pp. 24.
59. Bee Keeping. Pp. 48.
60. Methods of Curing Tobacco. Pp. 24.
61. Asparagus Culture. Pp. 40.
62. Marketing Farm Produce. Pp. 28.
64. Ducks and Geese. Pp. 54.
65. Experiment Station Work—II. Pp. 32.
66. Meadows and Pastures. Pp. 30.
68. The Black Rot of the Cabbage. Pp. 22.
69. Experiment Station Work—III. Pp. 32.
70. Insect Enemies of the Grape. Pp. 23.
71. Essentials in Beef Production. Pp. 24.
72. Cattle Ranges of the Southwest. Pp. 32.
73. Experiment Station Work—IV. Pp. 32.
74. Milk as Food. Pp. 39.
77. The Liming of Soils. Pp. 24.
78. Experiment Station Work—V. Pp. 32.
79. Experiment Station Work—VI. Pp. 28.
80. The Peach Twig-borer. Pp. 16.
81. Corn Culture in the South. Pp. 24.
82. The Culture of Tobacco. Pp. 24.
83. Tobacco Soils. Pp. 23.
84. Experiment Station Work—VII. Pp. 32.
85. Fish as Food. Pp. 32.
86. Thirty Poisonous Plants. Pp. 32.
87. Experiment Station Work—VIII. Pp. 32.
88. Alkali Lands. Pp. 23.
91. Potato Diseases and Treatment. Pp. 12.
92. Experiment Station Work—IX. Pp. 30.
93. Sugar as Food. Pp. 27.
95. Good Roads for Farmers. Pp. 46.
96. Raising Sheep for Mutton. Pp. 48.
97. Experiment Station Work—X. Pp. 32.
98. Suggestions to Southern Farmers. Pp. 48.
99. Insect Enemies of Shade Trees. Pp. 30.
100. Hog Raising in the South. Pp. 40.
101. Millets. Pp. 32.
102. Southern Forage Plants. Pp. 48.
103. Experiment Station Work—XI. Pp. 32.
104. Notes on Frost. Pp. 24.
105. Experiment Station Work—XII. Pp. 32.
106. Breeds of Dairy Cattle. Pp. 48.
107. Experiment Station Work—XIII. Pp. 32.
108. Saltbushes. Pp. 20.
109. Farmers' Reading Courses. Pp. 20.
110. Rice Culture in the United States. Pp. 28.
111. Farmer's Interest in Good Seed. Pp. 24.
112. Bread and Bread Making. Pp. 39.
113. The Apple and How to Grow It. Pp. 32.
114. Experiment Station Work—XIV. Pp. 28.
115. Hop Culture in California. Pp. 28.
116. Irrigation in Fruit Growing. Pp. 48.
118. Grape Growing in the South. Pp. 32.
119. Experiment Station Work—XV. Pp. 30.
120. Insects Affecting Tobacco. Pp. 32.
121. Beans, Peas, and other Legumes as Food. Pp. 38.
122. Experiment Station Work—XVI. Pp. 32.
124. Experiment Station Work—XVII. Pp. 32.
125. Protection of Food Products from Injurious Temperatures. Pp. 26.
126. Practical Suggestions for Farm Buildings. Pp. 48.
127. Important Insecticides. Pp. 46.
128. Eggs and Their Uses as Food. Pp. 38.
129. Sweet Potatoes. Pp. 40.
131. Household Tests for Detection of Oleomargarine and Renovated Butter. Pp. 11.
132. Insect Enemies of Growing Wheat. Pp. 40.
133. Experiment Station Work—XVIII. Pp. 32.
134. Tree Planting in Rural School Grounds. Pp. 32.
135. Sorghum Sirup Manufacture. Pp. 40.
136. Earth Roads. Pp. 24.
137. The Angora Goat. Pp. 48.
138. Irrigation in Field and Garden. Pp. 40.
139. Emmer: A Grain for the Semiarid Regions. Pp. 16.
140. Pineapple Growing. Pp. 48.
141. Poultry Raising on the Farm. Pp. 16.
142. Principles of Nutrition and Nutritive Value of Food. Pp. 48.
143. The Conformation of Beef and Dairy Cattle. Pp. 44.
144. Experiment Station Work—XIX. Pp. 32.
145. Carbon Bisulphid as an Insecticide. Pp. 28.
146. Insecticides and Fungicides. Pp. 16.
147. Winter Forage Crops for the South. Pp. 40.
148. Celery Culture. Pp. 32.
149. Experiment Station Work—XX. Pp. 32.
150. Clearing New Land. Pp. 24.
151. Dairying in the South. Pp. 48.
152. Scabies in Cattle. Pp. 32.
153. Orchard Enemies in the Pacific Northwest. Pp. 39.
154. The Home Fruit Garden: Preparation and Care. Pp. 16.
155. How Insects Affect Health in Rural Districts. Pp. 20.
156. The Home Vineyard. Pp. 24.
157. The Propagation of Plants. Pp. 24.
158. How to Build Small Irrigation Ditches. Pp. 28.
159. Scab in Sheep. Pp. 43.
161. Practical Suggestions for Fruit Growers. Pp. 30.
162. Experiment Station Work—XXI. Pp. 32.
164. Rape as a Forage Crop. Pp. 16.
165. Culture of the Silkworm. Pp. 32.
166. Cheese Making on the Farm. Pp. 16.
167. Cassava. Pp. 32.
168. Pearl Millet. Pp. 16.
169. Experiment Station Work—XXII. Pp. 32.
170. Principles of Horse Feeding. Pp. 44.
172. Scale Insects and Mites on Citrus Trees. Pp. 43.
173. Primer of Forestry. Pp. 48.
174. Broom Corn. Pp. 32.
175. Home Manufacture and Use of Unfermented Grape Juice. Pp. 16.
176. Cranberry Culture. Pp. 20.
177. Squab Raising. Pp. 32.
178. Insects Injurious in Cranberry Culture. Pp. 32.
179. Horseshoeing. Pp. 30.
181. Pruning. Pp. 39.

182. Poultry as Food. Pp. 40.
183. Meat on the Farm: Butchering, Curing, and Keeping. Pp. 37.
184. Marketing Live Stock. Pp. 40.
185. Beautifying the Home Grounds. Pp. 24.
186. Experiment Station Work—XXIII. Pp. 32.
187. Drainage of Farm Lands. Pp. 40.
188. Weeds Used in Medicine. Pp. 45.
190. Experiment Station Work—XXIV. Pp. 32.
192. Barnyard Manure. Pp. 32.
193. Experiment Station Work—XXV. Pp. 32.
194. Alfalfa Seed. Pp. 14.
195. Annual Flowering Plants. Pp. 48.
196. Usefulness of the American Toad. Pp. 16.
197. Importation of Game Birds and Eggs for Propagation. Pp. 30.
198. Strawberries. Pp. 24.
199. Corn Growing. Pp. 32.
200. Turkeys. Pp. 44.
201. Cream Separator on Western Farms. Pp. 23.
202. Experiment Station Work—XXVI. Pp. 32.
203. Canned Fruits, Preserves, and Jellies. Pp. 32.
204. The Cultivation of Mushrooms. Pp. 24.
205. Pig Management. Pp. 40.
206. Milk Fever and Its Treatment. Pp. 16.
208. Varieties of Fruits Recommended for Planting. Pp. 48.
209. Controlling the Boll Weevil in Cotton Seed and at Ginneries. Pp. 32.
210. Experiment Station Work—XXVII. Pp. 32.
211. The Use of Paris Green in Controlling the Cotton Boll Weevil. Pp. 23.
213. Raspberries. Pp. 38.
215. Alfalfa Growing. Pp. 40.
216. The Control of the Boll Weevil. Pp. 32.
217. Essential Steps in Securing an Early Crop of Cotton. Pp. 16.
218. The School Garden. Pp. 40.
219. Lessons from the Grain Rust Epidemic of 1904. Pp. 24.
220. Tomatoes. Pp. 32.
221. Fungous Diseases of the Cranberry. Pp. 16.
222. Experiment Station Work—XXVIII. Pp. 32.
223. Miscellaneous Cotton Insects in Texas. Pp. 24.
224. Canadian Field Peas. Pp. 16.
225. Experiment Station Work—XXIX. Pp. 32.
226. Relation of Coyotes to Stock Raising in the West. Pp. 24.
227. Experiment Station Work—XXX. Pp. 32.
228. Forest Planting and Farm Management. Pp. 22.
229. The Production of Good Seed Corn. Pp. 24.
231. Spraying for Cucumber and Melon Diseases. Pp. 24.
232. Okra: Its Culture and Uses. Pp. 16.
233. Experiment Station Work—XXXI. Pp. 32.
234. The Guinea Fowl. Pp. 24.
235. Preparation of Cement Concrete. Pp. 32.
236. Incubation and Incubators. Pp. 32.
237. Experiment Station Work—XXXII. Pp. 32.
238. Citrus Fruit Growing in the Gulf States. Pp. 48.
239. The Corrosion of Fence Wire. Pp. 32.
240. Inoculation of Legumes. Pp. 8.
241. Butter Making on the Farm. Pp. 32.
242. An Example of Model Farming. Pp. 16.
243. Fungicides and their Use in Preventing Diseases of Fruits. Pp. 32.
244. Experiment Station Work—XXXIII. Pp. 32.
245. Renovation of Worn-out Soils. Pp. 16.
246. Saccharine Sorghums for Forage. Pp. 37.
247. The Control of the Codling Moth and Apple Scab. Pp. 21.
248. The Lawn. Pp. 20.
249. Cereal Breakfast Foods. Pp. 36.
250. The Prevention of Stinking Smut of Wheat and Loose Smut of Oats. Pp. 16.
251. Experiment Station Work—XXXIV. Pp. 32.
252. Maple Sugar and Sirup. Pp. 36.
253. The Germination of Seed Corn. Pp. 16.
254. Cucumbers. Pp. 30.
255. The Home Vegetable Garden. Pp. 47.
256. Preparation of Vegetables for the Table. Pp. 48.
257. Soil Fertility. Pp. 39.
258. Texas or Tick Fever and its Prevention. Pp. 45.
259. Experiment Station Work—XXXV. Pp. 32.
260. Seed of Red Clover and Its Impurities. Pp. 24.
261. The Cattle Tick. Pp. 22.
262. Experiment Station Work—XXXVI. Pp. 32.
263. Practical Information for Beginners in Irrigation. Pp. 40.
264. The Brown-tail Moth and How to Control It. Pp. 22.
265. Game Laws for 1906. Pp. 54.
266. Management of Soils to Conserve Moisture.
267. Experiment Station Work—XXXVII. Pp. 32.
268. Industrial Alcohol: Sources and Manufacture. Pp. 45.
269. Industrial Alcohol: Uses and Statistics. Pp. 29.
270. Modern Conveniences for the Farm Home. Pp. 48.
271. Forage Crop Practices in Western Oregon and Western Washington. Pp. 39.
272. A Successful Hog and Seed Corn Farm. Pp. 16.
273. Experiment Station Work—XXXVIII. Pp 32.
274. Flax Culture. (In press.)

O

Printed by Libri Plureos GmbH in Hamburg, Germany